KAPPIYA'S KIDS ZONE

AKBAR & BIRBAL

KAPPIYA CLASSICS

Made with ♥ on the Notion Press Platform
www.notionpress.com

Contents

FOREWORD

KAPPIYA CLASSICS

Hello Dear Readers

I am Tamizhiniya Tamizhdesan

when I was studying in school my teachers used to conduct lessons between many good books and that conduct gave me confidence that I can conduct more than a hundred topics with introductory speech. My Technical education helped a lot in this aspect. When I became a teacher I assisted my students in the way our teachers guided us.

My school, college and workplace friends lives scattered in different countries like the poem of Eelam Poet V.I.S. Jayapalan, the families of them too scattered in different nation, whereas I live in the Land of my Mother Language(Tamilnadu). Among my friends who are running to strive for their living, I have selected the publishing department to read their lives and pass it on to others. We are publishing legendary works under Kappiya Vasipagam. So far we have published more than 1500 books in package type.

I have used the library a lot in my school, college and work life. Novelist Vasu Murugavel writes that he brought a bundle of books from a person, read them and returned them. Similarly, I have imported hundreds of books read them and sent them back. I have also written novel in Tamil and English, also a book based on the Culture of Tamil People.

My son Imayakappiyan (8) started learning his Tamil lettering from the texts of our cover pages. The same way he is gaining the knowledge of book names, authors also the technical knowledge in publishing and helps us in many ways. My husband Tamizhdesan guides me about the packaging materials of the book contents and his creative thinking of book cover page makes me to create some unique cover pages. We three feel very happy to be in this field which makes us to learn continuously.

I take great pleasure in publishing many of the war stories I have been reading. Movements that fight for the people are viewed by populists as scumbags. An example of this is the Tiger movement, which was not only similar to a government but also created various departments and the personality within them. There is no doubt that writing and reading them as well will diversify you.

I
WITTY 20

Introduction

Earlier, Emperor Akbar was ruling over the country. There was a great minister who was very wise, his name was Birbal. Birbal could answer any question properly. All questions were asked by Akbar to Birbal. Seeing the intimate relation between Akbar and Birbal, the prime minister and other ministers were jealous. There was one military officer who was very jealous of Birbal's intimacy with Akbar. He was the commander in chief of the army.

On a day when Birbal did not come to court, the commander-in-chief told Akbar, "O King! All of us are present here. We also have very good experience. You can get your doubts or questions answered by us. All the time you depend upon Birbal only. Give us one chance at least." Akbar came to the court. He looked at the whole court. Birbal was not there. "Where is Birbal?" he asked. Then the commander-in-chief got up and said, "Your majesty, you ask me the question. I shall answer. Ask me the question you would like to ask." Then all the scholars and ministers got up and said, "Your majesty, we are also here, give us a chance." Akbar got up. He addressed them and told them, "I will ask you a question. But you should satisfy me with your answer." The first question he asked, "In this world which is the best flower?" The commander-in-chief said, "Rose is the best flower". Prime minister said, "Jasmine is the best flower". Another said that Champak is the best. They went on discussing the qualities of different flowers. Akbar asked all of them to sit down.

The second question he asked, "Which milk is the best milk"? One person said cow's milk is the best milk. Another said goat's milk is the best milk. Each person went on saying some other milk is the best milk. "Sit down", Akbar said. "What is the sweetest thing in the world?" Akbar asked. Lot of them said jaggery. Some said honey. Some others said milk. Each person answered in his own way. Akbar was not satisfied. He asked them to sit down. Then he asked, "Which is the best leaf?" Somebody said coconut leaf is the best. Somebody said plantain leaf is the best. Each person named one leaf. "Sit down", Akbar commanded.

Then Birbal entered the court. He said, "Lord! I am here". "Did you hear my questions?", Akbar asked. Birbal said, "No". Then Akbar said, "Now I will ask you the questions, give me the answers. Which is the best flower in the world?" Without thinking, Birbal said, "Cotton flower is the best flower". "Why is it the best?" "Because cotton flowers give cotton? With cotton we make clothes, which protect us. Cotton flower is the most useful. You can smell other flowers once and then you have to throw them away. But the benefit of this cotton flower is permanent." Akbar was satisfied with the answer. "What is the second question?" "Which milk is the best milk?" For this Birbal said, "Mother's milk is the best milk. Because of mother's milk the child lives. Mother's milk nourishes the child. So mother's milk is the best milk."

Third question, "What is the sweetest thing in the world?" For this Birbal said, "Your majesty, sweet talk is the sweetest thing in the world. Not other things. Not milk, not honey and jaggery. A sweet word is the most valuable thing. With sweet words we can win a person. We can give great joy. You can attain higher status. When the crows caw we throw stones at them, whereas when the cuckoos sing we respect them. Neither is the cuckoo going to give us a crown nor is the crow going to punish us. When the tongue is good you can get a good name. Word is the sweetest thing in the world." Then the fourth question. "Which leaf is the best leaf?" Then Birbal said, "Betel leaf is the best leaf". He said, "Even before marriage, they exchange this leaf. On all auspicious occasions they give this Tambula (betel leaf). So betel leaf is the best leaf. Plantain leaf and coconut leaf are thrown away after use. Hence betel leaf is the most important leaf." The other people there were amazed at these answers.

Then the Emperor Akbar said, "The answers of the commander-in-chief, prime minister, etc. did not satisfy me. But Birbal's answers have satisfied me." Then Birbal saluted Akbar. All were seated. The court was completely silent. Emperor Akbar asked another question, "Birbal, there is no hair on my palm. Why is it like that?" Birbal gave the right answer, "Lord, all the time you are giving charity to many people. Your nature is to keep giving and giving. You keep on giving. The hand is used so much therefore no hair can grow there." Then Akbar asked, "All the people in the court are also not having hair on their palms?" Then Birbal said, "All the time they keep receiving things from you. You keep giving and they keep taking. Therefore no hair can grow on their palms also." Then Akbar asked, "There are many people who do not receive anything from me. They also do not have hair on their palms?" The Emperor wanted to give a good blow to his commander in chief and the prime minister. "The foolish people who cannot get things from you, the unfortunate people, they are jealous of people who get things from you. All the time they keep rubbing their palms out of jealousy and therefore hair is not growing in their palms also." All the people in the assembly were amazed. Then Akbar said, "Birbal, I do not know whether you are correct or not; but you have given me a satisfying answer. Your answers give joy and satisfaction to anyone who listens to your answer."

We need to talk in a manner which would satisfy others, which would give contentment to others, and which would give joy to others. Vedas, Shastras, Itihasas and Puranas are meant to give joy and satisfaction to others and not just for chanting alone.

1. *The Golden Gallows*

One day Akbar came to Court in a very bad mood. Unlike his true self, that day he snapped at several courtiers. The courtiers were apprehensive and sat quietly, till the Emperor left the Court.

Later when Birbal met Akbar in private, he asked him the reason for his anger. "Oh Birbal, do not ask! It is my son-in-law. The scoundrel is really annoying," Akbar was furious once again.

Birbal tried to calm him down, "Your Majesty, if you tell me what has happened, may be we could find a solution to the problem."

"Birbal, it has been a year since I saw my daughter. My son-in-law does not send her here to see us," complained Akbar.

"That is not such a big problem. I will send somebody right away to bring Your Majesty's daughter here," assured Birbal.

"You think I haven't already done that? My son-in-law is a stubborn man! He refuses to sent my daughter to me. I simply detest such son-in-law. Now there is something you must do for me, Birbal. Please arrange to put up gallows in the open grounds of the city. I will send all the son-in-laws in my kingdom to the gallows", announced Akbar, seething with rage.

Birbal couldn't believe his ears. How could the Emperor go to this extreme! He tried to pacify Akbar, but to no avail.

For the first time the situation was truly out of his hands. Birbal couldn't think of anything to stop Akbar. So he went to the city grounds and made arrangements for the gallows.

After a week the gallows were ready and Birbal took Akbar on an inspection tour. Akbar was quite pleased, "And now I can eliminate all the son-in-laws in my kingdom. What a relief!"

After a while, Akbar noticed a set of golden and silver gallows. "Birbal, may I ask for whom those special gallows are meant for?"

Birbal replied plainly, "The golden gallows are for you, Your Majesty. And the silver one is for me."

Bewildered, Akbar said, "I didn't ask you to do any such things. Why should we go to the gallows?"

Birbal replied, "Your Majesty, you wish to send all the son-in-laws in this kingdom to the gallows. Both of us are also the son-in-law of somebody. How can we exclude ourselves? Since you are the Emperor I arranged for a grand golden gallows for you. The silver one is for me, your Majesty. Don't you think it is appropriate?"

Akbar was amused and impressed by Birbal's wisdom. "What would I ever do without you Birbal," so saying he laughed. He realised his mistake and revoked the order.

2. *Birbal's Khichri*

On a cold winter day, Akbar and Birbal took a walk along the lake. A thought came into Birbal's mind that a man would do anything for money. He expressed his feelings to Akbar. The Emperor then put his fingers into the lake and immediately removed it because he shivered with cold.

Akbar said," I don't think a man would spend an entire night in the cold water of this lake for money."

Birbal replied,"I am sure I can find such a person."

Akbar then challenged Birbal to find such a person and said he would reward that person with a thousand gold coins.

Birbal searched far and wide until he found a poor man who was desperate enough to accept the challenge. The poor man entered the lake and Akbar had guards posted near him to make sure that he really did as promised.

The next morning the guards took the poor man to Akbar. The Emperor asked the poor man if he had indeed spent the night in the lake. The poor man replied that he did. Akbar then asked the poor man how he managed to spend the night in the lake. The poor man replied that there was a street lamp nearby and he kept his attention there on the lamp and away from the cold. Akbar then said that there would be no reward as the poor man had spent the night in the lake by the warmth of the street lamp. The poor man went to Birbal for help.

The next day, Birbal did not go to Court. Wondering where he was, Akbar sent a messenger to his home. The messenger came back saying that Birbal would come to Court once his Khichri was cooked. The Emperor waited for hours but Birbal did not come. Finally, Akbar decided to go to Birbal's house and see what he was up to.

He found Birbal sitting on the floor near some burning twigs and a utensil filled with kichri hanging five feet above the fire. The Emperor and his attendants couldn't help but laugh

Akbar then asked Birbal, "How can the khichri be cooked if it is so far away from the fire?"

Birbal answered, "The same way the poor man received heat from a street lamp that was more than a furlong away."

The Emperor realised his mistake and gave the poor man his reward.

3. Lost and Found

One day, when Akbar and Birbal were engaged in discussions, Birbal happened to pass a harmless comment about Akbar's sense of humour. But Emperor Akbar was in a foul mood and took great offence at this remark. He asked Birbal, his Court jester, friend and confidant, to not only leave the palace but also leave the precincts of the city of Agra. Birbal was terribly hurt at being banished.

A couple of days later, Akbar began to miss his best friend. He regretted his earlier decision of banishing him from the Court. He just could not do without Birbal and so sent out a search party to look for him. But Birbal had left town without letting anybody know of his destination. The soldiers searched high and low but were unable to find him anywhere.

Then one day a wise saint visited the palace accompanied by two of his disciples. The disciples claimed that their teacher was the wisest man to walk the earth. Since Akbar was missing Birbal terribly he thought it would be a good idea to have a wise man who could keep him company. But he decided that he would first ascertain the holy man's wisdom.

The saint had bright sparkling eyes, a thick beard and long hair. The next day, when they came to visit the Court, Akbar informed the holy man that since he was the wisest man on earth, he would like to test him. All his ministers would put forward a question and if his answers were satisfactory, he would be made a minister. But if he failed, he would be beheaded. The saint answered that he had never claimed to the wisest man on earth,even though other people seemed to think so. Nor was he eager to display his wisdom, but as he enjoyed answering questions, he was ready for the test.

One of the ministers, Raja Todar Mal, began the round of questioning. He asked, "Who is man's best friend on earth?" To which the wise saint replied,"His own good sense."

Next Faizi asked which was the most superior thing on earth? "Knowledge", answered the saint.

"Which is the deepest trench in the world?" asked Abul Fazl. And the saint answered, "A woman's heart."

"What is that which cannot be regained after it is lost?" questioned another courtier and the reply he received was: "Life".

"What is undying in music?" asked Court musician Tansen. The saint replied: "Notes". And then Tansen asked, " Which is the sweetest and most melodious voice at night-time?" and the answer received was:"The voice that prays to God."

Maharaja Mansingh of Jaipur - who was a guest at the palace - asked, "What travels more speedily than the wind?" The saint replied that it was "Man's thought." Mansingh then asked, "Which is the sweetest thing on the earth?" and the saint said that it was a "Baby's smile".

Emperor Akbar and all his courtiers were very impressed with his answers,but Akbar wanted to test the saint himself. First,he asked what were the necessary requirements to rule over a kingdom, for which he received the response "Cleverness". Then he asked what was the greatest enemy of a king. The saint replied it was "Selfishness".

The Emperor was pleased and offered the saint a seat of honour and asked him whether he could perform any miracle. The saint said that he could manifest any person the Emperor wished to meet.Akbar was thrilled and immediately asked to meet his minister and best friend Birbal.

The saint simply pulled off his artificial beard and hair much to the surprise of the courtiers. Akbar was stunned and could not believe his eyes. He stepped down to embrace the saint because he was none other than Birbal!

Akbar had tears in his eyes as he told Birbal that he has suspected it was him and had therefore asked whether he could perform miracles. He showered Birbal with many valuable gifts to show him how happy he was at his return.

4. *The Effects of Your Actions*

One day Akbar was simply chatting with his friends. He had around him the very best, wisest, most creative people chosen from every part of the country. They were speaking, Akbar all of the sudden slapped Birbal for no apparent reason. Now one could slap the Emperor back, but the slap had to go somewhere.

So Birbal slapped the person who was standing right next to him.

Everybody thought, "This is strange!"

There was no reason in the first place for Akbar's slap.

Suddenly, as if some madness had seized Akbar, he has slapped poor Birbal. And the victim also reacted strangely. Rather than asking, "Why have you slapped me?" he simply slapped the man by his side! and that man, thinking perhaps this was the norm at the Court, slapped the next person. In a chain reaction, the slap went all around the Court.

That night, Akbar's wife slapped him! and he asked, "Why are you slapping me?"

She said," What a question - a Game is a Game."

He asked, "Who told you that this is a game?"

We have been hearing the whole day long that a great game has begun in the Court. The only rule is that you cannot hit the person back, you have to find somebody else to slap. And somebody has slapped me, so your slap has come back to you. The game is now complete!"

5. *Poet Raidas*

In the town of Agra lived a rich businessman. But he was also a miser. Various people used to flock outside his house everyday hoping for some kind of generosity, but they always had to return home disappointed. He used to ward them off with false promises, never living up to his word.

Then one day, a poet named Raidas arrived at his house and said that he wanted to read out his poems to the rich man. As the rich man was very fond of poetry, he welcomed him with open arms.

Raidas then recited all his poems one by one. The richman was very pleased and especially so when he heard the poem that Raidas had written on him, because he had been compared with Kubera, the God of Wealth. In those days it was a custom for rich men and kings to show their appreciation through a reward or gift, as that was the only means of earning for a poor poet. So the rich man promised Raidas some gifts and asked him to come and collect them the next day. Raidas was pleased.

The next morning when the poet arrived at the house, the rich man pretended that he had never laid eyes on him before. When Raidas reminded him of his promise, he said that although Raidas was a good poet he understood very little of human nature. And that if a rich businessman like him truly wanted to reward the poet, he would have done so the very same night. Raidas had been offered a reward not because he was really pleased or impressed, but simply to encourage him.

Raidas was extremely upset, but as there was nothing that he could do, he quietly left the house. On his way home he saw Birbal riding a horse. So he stopped him and asked for his help after narrating the whole incident.

Birbal took him to his house in order to come up with a plan. After giving it some thought he asked Raidas to go to a friend's house and request the friend to plan a dinner on the coming full moon night, where the rich man would also be invited. Birbal then asked Raidas to relax and leave the rest to him.

Raidas had a trusted friend whose name was Mayadas. So he went up to him and told him the plan. The next day, Mayadas went to the rich man's house and invited him for dinner. The dinner had been planned for the coming full moon night. Mayadas said that he intended to serve his guests in vessels of gold, which the guests would get to take home after the meal. The rich man was thrilled to hear this and jumped at the offer.

After sunset on the full moon night, the rich man arrived at Mayadas house and was surprised to see no other guests there except Raidas. Anyway, they welcomed him and began a polite conversation. The rich man had come on a empty stomach and so was getting hungrier by the minute. Raidas and Mayadas were quite full, as they had eaten just before the rich man's arrival.

Finally, at midnight, the rich man could bear his hunger no longer and asked Mayadas to serve the food. Mayadas sounded extremely surprised and asked him what food he was talking about! Then rich man tried to remind him that he had been invited for dinner. At that point Raidas asked him for proof of the invitation. The rich man had no answer. Then Mayadas told him that he had just invited him to please him and had not really meant it. He then went on to say that even though they did not do anything good for other people, they also would never try to hurt another human being. He asked the rich man not to feel bad.

At that point Birbal walked into the room and reminded the rich man of the same treatment that he had himself meted out to Raidas. The rich man realised his mistake and begged for forgiveness. He said that Raidas was a good poet and had not asked him for any reward. He himself had promised to give him some gifts and then cheated him out of them. To make up for his mistake he took out the necklace that he was wearing and gifted it to Raidas. Then they all sat down to eat a healthy meal.

Raidas was all praise for Birbal and thanked him profusely. Emperor Akbar also invited Raidas to his Court and honoured him.

6. *Self Publicity*

One day a Brahmin by the name of Sevaram asked Birbal for help. He said that his forefathers were great Sanskrit scholars and that people used to respectfully refer to them as Panditji. He said that he had no money nor need for wealth; he was content living a simple life. But he had just one wish. He wished people would refer to him as Panditji too. He asked Birbal how he could achieve this.

Birbal said that the task was fairly simple. If the Brahmin followed his advice word for word, this task could be achieved. Birbal advised the Brahmin to shout at anyone who called him Panditji from now on.

Now the children who lived in the same street as the Brahmin, did not like him since he scolded them often. They were just waiting for an opprtunity to get back at him. Birbal told the children that the Brahmin would get really irritated if they started calling him Pandiji. So the children began to tease him by yelling,"Panditji" whenever he appeared and, as advised by Birbal, the Brahmin responded by shouting at them. The children spread the word to all the other children in the neighbourhood that Sevaram hated being called Panditji, so they too joined in the chorus, calling him Panditji.

After a while, Sevaram got tired of scolding them but by now everyone was used to calling him Panditji. Hence the game was over but the name stuck!

7. Greater than God?

One day, two poets from a faraway kingdom arrived at Akbar's Court. They delighted everyone with their songs and poems. The Emperor, who was always generous, rewarded them well. The poets had never seen so much gold before. They were overwhelmed. Then the Emperor ordered that they be given a set of princely clothes each.

Then one of the poets begged permission to offer a poem of thanks. Emperor Akbar nodded and the poet began his recitation. He spoke of the Emperor's bravery and kindness. He praised the Emperor's learning and wisdom.

He ended by saying that Emperor Akbar was the greatest king that had ever ruled. "Over this world or any other, He is greater than God Himself." With that, the poet bowed and left the hall.

There was a moment of silence. Many of those in the hall were shocked that the poet had compared a mortal to God.

Emperor Akbar looked around and his eyes began to twinkle mischievously. "So," he said, "it appears that I am now even greater than God."

All the people in the hall looked at their Emperor in horror. Had he really believed the poet's words" Surely not! And yet, they were not entirely sure. Emperor Akbar looked at his ministers and commanders, his nobles and his counsellors. He wondered if any of them would have the courage to speak the truth. The ministers, commanders, nobles and counsellors looked back at him. Nobody stirred.

"So," said the Emperor, beginning to feel irritated, "everyone present agrees that your Emperor is greater than God."

Nobody dared to disagree. Slowly, one by one, the courtiers bowed to show that they agreed. A low, shamed murmur of "Yes, Your Majesty," "It is so, Your Majesty," filled the hall.

Emperor Akbar thought that the courtiers were acting very foolishly. He turned to Birbal with a frown. "And you, Birbal. Do you agree too?" he asked.

"Oh, yes," Birbal replied immediately.

The Emperor's frown grew.

"Your Majesty, you can do something even God cannot!" Birbal said. "If any of your subjects displeases you, Your Majesty, you can send him on a pilgrimage or banish him from your empire, never to return. But God cannot. For God rules over the entire earth ant the sky and the heavens. There is no place in this world or any other that does not belong to God. So he cannot banish any of His creature."

Emperor Akbar's frown vanished. "Well said, Birbal!" he cried delightedly. And, from every corner of the Court, relieved courtiers began to smile weakly and then laugh. Birbal had done it again!

8. Controversial Brinjal

Emperor Akbar was discussing about brinjals with Birbal. He told him what a delicious and nutritious vegetable it was. Much to Akbar's surprise, Birbal thoroughly agreed with him and even sang two songs in praise of the humble brinjal.

After a couple of days, the royal chef cooked brinjal curry for lunch. Birbal was also eating at the palace that day. When the brinjal curry was served to Akbar, he refused it saying that it was a tasteless, stale vegetable, full of seeds and lacking proper nutrition. He then asked that it be served to Birbal who loved brinjals.

But Birbal too, refused it impatiently saying that it was not good for health. So, Akbar asked him why he was saying such things, when he had actually sung the brinjal's praise only a few days ago.

Birbal replied that he had praised the brinjal only because his Emperor had praised it and criticised it when His Majesty had criticised it, as he was loyal to his Emperor and not to the brinjal! Birbal said, the brinjal could not make him a minister, no matter how much he praised it.

The Emperor was pleased by the bold and witty response.

9. The Holy Book

Akbar once called Birbal and said to him, "Birbal it is said in one of your Hindu Holy Books that Lord Vishnu one day heard the agonised cry of one of His elephants and rushed to his aid. Why would a God with so many servants at his disposal, himself rush to the succour of the elephant?"

Birbal replied, "Your Majesty, give me few days to answer your question."
The Emperor granted him the request.

Birbal made a wax model of the Emperor's grandson and dressed him up in the grandson's clothes. He then told the servant in charge of the grandson to carry the doll out where the Emperor could see him and pretend to fall to the ground and throw the doll into the pond nearby, uttering a cry to draw the Emperor's attention. "If you do so, I shall reward you greatly."

The servant followed Birbal's instruction threw the doll into the pond and himself pretended to fall to the ground, uttering a plaintive cry.

When the Emperor heard the cry and saw his grandson fall into the pond, he rushed and jumped into the pond to rescue him.

Birbal stepped out of the bushes and lent a helping hand to the Emperor as he came out of the pond, asking him, "How did Your Majesty jump to the rescue of your grandson when you have so many servants to do this job for you? For the same reason Lord Vishnu rushes to save whoever seeks His help, because in his eyes all creatures are equally precious."

10. *The Pot of Intelligence*

Hello Children! Here comes one more interesting story for you.

Akbar had great confidence in Birbal. But once, for some unknown reason, the Emperor was not very happy with him. Sensing this, Birbal decided to stay away from the Emperor for few days. He went to a small village and started living there.

One day, Akbar got a letter. One of his vassals, Raja Samant, had written, "Please send me a pot full of intelligence."

Akbar could not comprehend what it meant. He thought," If only Birbal was here, he would have explained it in a minute."

The Emperor came up with an idea to find out where Birbal might be. He invited the heads of the village and said, "I shall give a goat to each one of you. You must feed them well. Take good care of them. The cost is my responsibility. You must return the goats after one month. But when you return, the goats should weigh the same as they are today."

The village heads wondered how this would be possible.

Somehow, Birbal came to know about this. He went to see the Patel (village head).

"Patelji, do not worry about what the Emperor has said. Just take good care of the goat," said Birbal.

"In that case, the goat will grow fat."

"There is a solution for that. On the outskirts of the village, there is a lion in the cage. Tie up this goat just a little way of from the lion. Due to fear and insecurity, the goat will not gain an ounce of weight," said Birbal.

The Patel followed Birbal's instruction. After a month all goats were brought to the Emperor. Only one goat had not gained any weight. Akbar guessed that this was possible only with Birbal's help. He sent for Birbal and pacified him. Then he said, "Birbal, I need your advice. How can I sent a pot full of intelligence to someone?"

Birbal started working on it. First, he got a pot, filled it with soil and sowed a pumpkin seed in it. It sprouted and a pumpkin grew inside the pot. When the pumpkin filled the pot, Birbal cut of the plant. The pumpkin remained inside the pot. Birbal tied a cloth and covered the pot. He showed this to Akbar.

"O Sire, send this to Raja Samant with a letter. Say, this is full of intelligence. Take it out carefully. While removing the pumpkin, the pot should not break and the container should not get damaged. If anything contrary to this happens, you will have to pay a very heavy penalty."

The vassal received the pot and the letter. He realised what an impossible task it was. He came to Akbar's Court and apologised. He realised what a fool he was to ask for a pot of intelligence from an Emperor in whose kingdom a man like Birbal lived!"

11. *The Pandit's Pot*

A Pandit once went to Akbar's Court and told the Emperor he would like to test the intelligence of his Courtiers. Akbar gave him permission. The Courtiers gathered in the palace at the appointed hour. The Pandit kept a covered pot before them and asked them to tell him what it contained.

There was absolute silence. Then Birbal stepped forward, he uncovered the pot and said there was nothing in it.

"But you opened it!" said the Pandit.

"You did not say we should not open it," replied Birbal. The Pandit was disappointed. He bowed to the Emperor and walked away.

12. *The Well Water*

A farmer and his neighbor, once went to Emperor Akbar's Court with a complaint.

"Your Majesty, I bought a well from him," said the farmer pointing to his neighbor, " and now he wants me to pay for the water."

"That's right, Your Majesty," said the neighbor. "I sold him the well but not the water".

The Emperor asked Birbal to settle the dispute.

"Didn't you say that you sold your well to this farmer?" Birbal asked the neighbor. "So the well belongs to him now, but you have kept your water in his well. Is that right? Well, in that case you will have to pay him rent or take your water out at once."

The neighbor realised that he was out witted. He quickly apologised and gave up his claim.

13. Retrieving the Ring

Once Akbar threw his gold ring into a dry well and asked his minister's to retrieve it without climbing down into the well.

The ministers scratched their heads and thought deeply but soon had to admit defeat. Birbal, however, could never resist a challenge.

"Your Majesty, you shall get back your ring by sundown", he declared.

Birbal took some fresh cow-dung from the ground and threw it on top of the ring. He tied a stone to one end of a long piece of string and retaining the other end, threw the stone on the dung. After a while, when he felt sure that the cow-dung had dried completely, he pulled the string up. To everyone's surprise the cow-dung came up and stuck at the bottom was Emperor's ring.

14. Akbar's Dream

One night, Emperor Akbar dreamt that he had lost all his teeth except one. The next morning, he invited all the astrologers of his kingdom to interpret this dream.

After long discussion, the astrologers prophesied that all the Emperor's relatives would die before him.

Akbar was very upset by this interpretation and sent away all the astrologers without any reward. Later that day, Birbal entered the Court. Akbar related his dream and asked him to interpret it.

After thinking for a while, Birbal replied that the Emperor would live a longer and more fulfilled life than any of his relatives.

Akbar was pleased with Birbal's explanation and rewarded him handsomly.

15. The Glutton

Akbar had a real passion for food. In his royal kitchen were employed all kinds of master chefs, who made a variety of gourmet dishes. Often Akbar would throw a banquet for his courtiers to enjoy these meals in the palace gardens.

Once at one such banquet Birbal was seated next to Emperor Akbar. After the meal, bowls of pistachios were served to all. Both Birbal and Akbar went on eating the pistachios and they threw the shells under their chairs.

Soon there was heaps of pistachio shells under their chairs. Akbar saw the heaps and thought of playing a trick on Birbal. He thought to himself, "For once let me outwit the clever Birbal."

Quitely, Akbar pushed his heap of shells under Birbal's chair with his foot. Birbal did not notice him do this. All of a sudden Akbar sprang from his chair and with a bewildered look he said aloud, "I don't believe this Birbal! How could you eat so many pistachios? You are really a glutton!"

All the courtiers heard this and looked at the big heap of pistachio shells under Birbal's chair. But Birbal was unperturbed; he knew that Akbar had played a trick on him. But the clever Birbal could not allow the Emperor and the courtier's to ridicule him.

Promptly, he said to Akbar, "Your Majesty, You are absolutely right, I am a glutton. It is true that I have eaten a lot of pistachios. But Your Majesty, you really surprised me! How could you eat the pistachios along with the shells?"

Birbal requested the courtiers to look under Akbar's chair. They did not see a single shell there and neither were there any shells in his bowls. The courtiers burst out laughing.

Akbar turned red in face. He had attempted to trick Birbal and in the end himself became the butt of ridicule!

Although truly embarrassed, he gently appreciated Birbal's wit and humor.

16. Call him at Once

One morning Akbar woke up early. Rubbing his fingers over his stubble he called out, "Is anyone there? Quick! Call him at once!"

The guard outside his chamber was thoroughly confused. He thought to himself, "Whom is the Emperor calling, he didn't name anybody in particular. The guard was too frightened to ask the Emperor to repeat his order.

The guard sought the help of another guard. That guard in turn spoke to a third. The third mentioned it to a fourth. Finally all the guards inside the palace knew of the Emperor's order. There was utter confusion, as nobody knew whom the Emperor had called for.

At that time Birbal happened to be taking a walk in the garden. Seeing the guards in total confusion, he guessed the Emperor must have made a strange request. He called one of the guards and asked him "What is the matter? Why are all the guards running around confused?"

The guard told Birbal about the Emperor's order. He said, "His Majesty has not mentioned anyone in particular. Whom should we call? We do not know what to do. If we do not get anyone, the Emperor will be very annoyed with us. What shall we do, Sir?"

"Hmmm! Tell me what the Emperor was doing when he gave the order" asked Birbal. The attendant pondered a while, "Nothing unusual Sir, he was just rubbing the stubble on his chin."

Birbal smiled, for he knew whom the Emperor wanted. He said to the guard, "Take the barber to the Emperor immediately".

The guard called the barber and took him immediately to the Emperor. The Emperor thought to himself, "How come the barber is here? I did not mention anyone in particular."

The Emperor asked the guard, "Tell me, was it your idea to call the barber or did someone help you?"

"Your Majesty, it was Birbal's suggestion," said the guard.

Once again Akbar was impressed with Birbal's wisdom.

17. Theft of Jewels

A merchant in Akbar's kingdom felt hot and decided to have a bath. He bundled up all the jewels he was wearing let them in a corner of his room along with his clothes and went for a bath. When he came out from his bath, he discovered that his jewels had vanished. He questioned all his servants but was unable to discover who had stolen the jewels. He decided to go to

Akbar to have his problem solved. Akbar assigned the case to Birbal. Birbal called the merchant and asked him to bring all his servants to the Court next day.

When they appeared before him, Birbal handed each of the servants a stick and told them: "I have given each of you a stick of the same length. But they are magic sticks. Whenever they are in the possession of a thief they grow exactly by one inch a day. If you have stolen Your Masters jewels, your stick will grow by one inch when you come back tomorrow. So take them home and bring them back here tomorrow, at the same time." He then dismissed the servants.

The next day when the Court had assembled and the merchant's servants arrived with their sticks, Birbal collected all the sticks placed them next to each other. One stick was shorter by one inch. Birbal told the merchant, "The servant who brought this stick is the one who stole the jewels. He cut the stick so it would not show that it grew by one inch and he would not be caught".

He then told servants, "These are not magic sticks, but because you believed that they were, the guilty servant cut an inch off his stick".

Immediately, the servant who had stolen the jewels confessed and returned them.

18. *List of Fools*

One day an Arab merchant arrived at the court of Akbar with a large consignment of horses of all ages and breeds and offered them for sale.

Akbar was very impressed with the quality of the horses, paid up the prices demanded for the ones he selected and ordered the merchant to send him some more of the best that he could find in Arabia. The merchant agreed and demanded an advance sum of Rs.2 lakhs for them. Akbar immediately ordered the Court treasurer to pay the amount and the merchant left promising to return as soon as he had acquired the horses, which had been ordered.

Some time later, Akbar asked Birbal to prepare a list of fools in his kingdom. Birbal replied, "Your Majesty, I have already made one" and handed him a long list. Akbar was astonished to find his own name headed the list.

Outraged, he shouted at Birbal, "How dare you put Your Emperor's name in the list of fools!"

Birbal replied evenly, "Last week Your Majesty gave Rs.2 lakhs to the Arab merchant without any guarantee that he would bring you the horses that you ordered and paid for. That justifies me putting your name at the top of the list of Fools"

Akbar asked him, "What if the merchant brings me the horses which I have ordered?"

"Then Your Majesty, I will replace Your name with his".

Akbar realised he had made a mistake in advancing the money and remained silent.

19. All For The Best

Birbal constantly asserted that everything happens for one's own good. Emperor Akbar, who was young, was distrustful of Birbal's wisdom and questioned the minister's constant, optimistic assertion.

One day while handling a sword, the Emperor chopped off the tip of his little finger. Birbal immediately told the Emperor not to worry, everything that happens has a purpose behind it and that purpose is for good. The Emperor became exceedingly angry with Birbal and threw him in jail.

The Emperor bandaged the little finger for few days and then as a diversion, went into the forest to hunt. He was later separated from his hunting party and eventually captured by a tribe of cannibals intending to make human sacrifice. The Emperor was bound like a sacrifice lamb and taken before the temple.When the temple priest examined him, the priest announced that he could not be sacrificed because he was not a perfect specimen,since the front portion of one finger was missing. As he was not fit to be sacrificed, the Emperor was released.

On his return, the Emperor thanked God for injuring his finger and thereby sparing his life then immediately went to the prison to meet Birbal.

"O, Birbal", please accept my apologies for imprisoning you. Now I understand how my injury was for the best. But tell me why did God allow me to imprison you? How is it for the best that you have been confines here due to my angry?

Birbal replied," Your Majesty, if I had not been in prison, you would surely have taken me with you when you went for hunting, and when the forest cannibals rejected you for their sacrifice, they would surely have found me an excellent substitute!"

20. *Birbal's Journey To Paradise*

The Akbar Court barber nursed his hatred for Birbal and plotted against him daily. One day he stuck upon a plan and so,when Emperor Akbar next called him to trim his beard,he said: "You know, Your Majesty,last night I dreamed about your Father".

The Great Mughal at once showed interest, "Tell me what he said to you".

"He said he is very happy in paradise,but he says that all the inhabitants of Heaven are terrible bores. He would like you to send someone who can talk to him and keep him amused".

Of course, no one possessed wit like Birbal and although Akbar prized him very much, to appear his poor father in Paradise, he would consent to give him up. Naturally, the only way of reaching Heaven is through Death.

When Birbal responded to the Emperor's summons, Akbar said : "I think you love me enough, Birbal, to make any sacrifice or my sake".

"You know I do Your Majesty" Birbal said.

"Then I would like you to go to Heaven and keep my dear Father company".

"Very Well", Birbal said, "but please give me few days to prepare".

"Certainly", said the Mughal, delighted, "You are doing me a great favour". "I will give you a week time".

Birbal went home and dug a deep pit,which would serve as his own grave.But he also excavated a secret tunnel that opened under the floor of his house,then he returned to the Emperial Court.

"Your Highness" he said, "in accordance with an old family tradition,I would like to be buried near my house and. if you don't mind,I would like to die by being buried alive. It is easier to get into Heaven that way, you know".

So, to the great happiness of the court barber, Birbal was buried alive. Ofcourse he made his way at once through the tunnel into his own house,were he stayed in concealment for over six months.

At the end of that time, with his hair and beard grown long and shaggy, he came out of hiding, and obtained an audience with the Great Mughal.

"Birbal" cried the Emperor. "Where have you come from?"

"From Paradise,Your Majesty. I spent such a lovely time with your Father that he gave me special permission to return to earth".

"Did he give you any message or his Son?"

"Just one,Your Highness, Do you see my whiskers and long hair? Well, it seems very few barbers make it to Heaven. Your Father asks you to send him yours at once".

21. Finding The Right Balance

Once it happened that Birbal and Akbar exchanged some hot words and Birbal took off in anger.

After a few days the Emperor cooled down and realized that he had treated Birbal unjustly. Also he was missing Birbal's scintillating wit and his intelligence in solving the daily issues in the court.

But even though the emperor was ready to call Birbal back the problem was that Birbal had left no forwarding address. He had simply disappeared. Also, Akbar didn't want to have to apologize to Birbal even though he wanted him back.

Having lived in Birbal's company for so long, the Emperor had also gained some craftiness. He devised a plan that would find Birbal without having to make an announcement that would give away Akbar's eagerness to have Birbal back.

Soon, all the district Sarpanch's in the kingdom received a goat from the Emperor. With the goat was a message - the goat was the property of Emperor Akbar and was being entrusted to the district for safekeeping for a month. The goat must be well taken care of and returned at the end of the month. The most important thing was that the goat must not gain any weight during the month nor should it lose any weight.

Sarpanch after sarpanch watched as the messengers from the Royal Court weighed a got in front of him and told him that it should be the same weight 30 days later, within a reasonable limit.

And once the messengers were gone, the Sarpanch invariably scratched his head. The message from the Royal Court was as baffling as it was clear. The whole thing sounded like a riddle.

Even though a huge crowd collected on each site to watch the sight of a goat being put in a balance, no citizen had any ideas to keep the goat's weight constant.

I am sure some smartasses would have suggested sending it to a slimming clinic had such been invented back then.

Some villages tried smart methods like feeding the goat for fifteen days and then not feeding at all for the remaining fortnight and other variations. Invariably the goat either died or lost weight. In some cases the goat actually gained weight.

On the 30th day, there was only one goat that weight almost exactly the same as a month ago. The Emperor was extremely interested in that goat. He found out which district the goat had been sent to and went there immediately.

On questioning from the Supreme Ruler himself, the Sarpanch gave up the secret - "Sire, we fed the goat very well, as the rations were kindly provided by the Zille-ilahi, but after a day's feeding the goat was then taken away and tied in front of the tiger's cage for the night."

Akbar smiled at the clever solution. Fear of the tiger would counteract all the goat's feeding without starving it. It was ingenious! Then the Emperor asked the million-dollar question - "Who told you this solution?"

The Sarpanch gave the name of the wise villager who had saved the Sarpanch from going crazy with the insoluble puzzle and in a short amount of time Birbal was standing in front of Akbar accepting Akbar's weak apologies with a tolerant smile.

22. *Half The Reward*

Once when Akbar went hunting in the jungle, he lost his way. Mahesh Das who lived in the outskirts helped the king reach the palace. The emperor rewarded him with his ring.

The Emperor also promised to give him a responsible posting at his court. After a few days Mahesh Das went to the court. The guard did not allow him to enter.

Mahesh Das showed the guard the ring which the king had given him. Now the guard thought that the young man was sure to get more rewards by the king. The greedy guard agreed to allow him inside the court on one condition. It was that Mahesh Das had to pay him half the reward he would get from the Emperor. Mahesh Das accepted the condition.

He then entered the court and showed the ring to the King.

The King who recognized Mahesh asked him "Oh young man! What do you expect as a reward from the King of Hindustan?" "Majesty! I expect 50 lashes from you as a reward." replied Mahesh Das. The courtiers were stunned. They thought that he was mad. Akbar pondered over his request and asked him the reason.

Mahesh Das said he would tell him the reason after receiving his reward. Then the king's men whipped him as per his wish. After the 25th lash Mahesh Das requested the King to call the guard who was at the gate.

The guard appeared before the King. He was happy at the thought that he was called to be rewarded. But to his surprise, Mahesh Das told the King ,"Jahampana! This greedy guard let me inside on condition that I pay him half the reward I receive from you. I wanted to teach him a lesson. Please give the remaining 25 lashes to this guard so that I can keep my promise to him."

The King then ordered that the guard be given 25 lashes along with 5 years of imprisonment. The King was very happy with Mahesh Das. He called him RAJA BIRBAL and made him his chief minister.

II

TINY 30

1. INTRODUCTION

Emperor Akbar loved to go hunting. On one such trip, he came across a young man named Mahesh Das. In the meeting that occurred, the Emperor was extremely impressed by the wit of Mahesh Das. The Emperor gave Mahesh Das his ring and asked him to come and visit him in his palace at any time.

A few years later Mahesh Das decided to try his luck in the city and to take the emperor up on his offer. He reached the city of Agra where Emperor Akbar had his fort on the banks of the Yamuna River. At the gate of the fort he was greeted by the guards. He told them that he had come to visit with the emperor.

The guards looked at him in disdain (since he was not very well dressed) and asked him why they should let him in. He showed them the ring that was given to him by the emperor as proof. One of the guards realized that this individual obviously was of importance to the emperor and gave him permission to enter, based on one condition:the young man would share half of what he received from the emperor with the guard.

Mahesh Das promised to do so and was given access into the court of Emperor Akbar. He bowed to the emperor as he went in and showed him the ring. The reputedly benevelont Emperor Akbar recognized the ring and the young man and immediately offered him anything he wanted. The young man thought a while, and asked the emperor for fifty lashes of the whip.

The emperor was amazed but he knew that Mahesh Das was a very astute young man and asked him for his reason for his wish. Mahesh Das revealed to the emperor that deal that he had made with the guard outside the fort. The emperor was thoroughly amused and angry at the same time. He awarded the fifty lashes to the guard for his impertinence and his habit of bullying people.

He rewarded Mahesh Das by including him in his court and giving him all the comforts he could desire. He also bestowed on him the name of Birbal.

2. Birbal catches a thief

Birbal was one of the nine gems in the court of emperor Akbar. He was respected by everyone for his intelligence and wit. Whenever Akbar was in difficulty, he called Birbal for help.

Akbar was very fond of jewellery. He had many rings of gold, pearls and diamonds. His favourite ring was the one with a large diamond at the centre and pearls around.

At the emperor's palace, there were eight servants who looked after his clothes and jewellery. They also helped him get ready to go to the court. No one else was allowed to enter his room.

One day, the Emperor wanted to wear his favourite ring. But it was missing. Akbar ordered a search for the ring. But no one could find it.

Akbar then asked his men to call Birbal. When Birbal came, he told him about the robbery and asked for help. Birbal called all the eight servants who were in charge of the Emperor's room.

He gave each of them a stick of the same size and asked them to come back with it the next day. He told them that the stick of the person who had stolen the ring would become longer by one inch that night.

The next morning, the eight servants stood in a line with their sticks. Birbal caught hold of one of them and took him to Akbar.

The man fell at Akbar's feet and admitted that he had stolen the ring.

The king was surprised. He asked Birbal how he found out the culprit. Birbal said the thief had cut his stick by an inch fearing that it would grow.

3. Back to Square One

As usual a lot of people were present in Akbar's durbar. A famous astrologer had come from a far away country.

He was talking about the Solar System and the Earth's shape.

At one point Akbar said, "If the earth is round, and if one travel strait towards one direction, he will come back to the same spot from where he has started the journey."

"Theoretically it is correct", said the astrologer.

"Why not in real life?", asked the king.

"One has to cross oceans, mountains and forests to keep the path straight." the astrologer said.

"Sail through the oceans, make tunnels in the mountains and use elephants to cross the forests." Akbar found the solution.

"Still it is impossible" said the astrologer.

"Why?" Asked Akbar.

"It may take years to complete the whole journey" said the astrologer

"Years? How many?" asked Akbar.

"I don't know. May be a hundred years or more" said the astrologer

"Don't worry I will ask my ministers. They have an answer for everything" Akbar looked at the ministers.

"Impossible to calculate"

"Around 25 years"

"Fifty years or less"

"80 days"

"Why Birbal, you haven't uttered a word" the king showed his surprise at Birbal's silence.

"I was just calculating the time required to go round the earth" explained Birbal.

"And did you get the answer?" asked the king.

"Sure." Said Birbal "It will take just one day."

"Just one day! Birbal, it is Impossible! Even it will take more than one day to cross our country." Said Akbar.

"It is possible. Provided you travel at the speed of the Sun" said Birbal with a smile.

4. The Blind Saint

There lived a saint in an ashram in the kingdom of Emperor Akbar.

He was believed to prophecy the future correctly, despite being a blind man.

Once he had a visitor who had come to treat their niece. The child's parents were killed in front of the girl's eyes.

Once she saw the saint, she started to scream loudly saying that that saint was the culprit. Angered by the girl's words the saint demanded the couple to get away with their child.

The whole day the girl cried which made the couple to realize that the girl was not lying. Therefore, they decided to seek the help of Raja Birbal.

Birbal consoled them and asked them to wait at the Emperor's assembly. Birbal had invited the saint to Akbar's court too.

Then in front of all the ministers he drew a sword and neared the saint to kill him. The saint in bewilderment immediately drew another sword and began to fight.

Thus by this act of the saint it was proved that he was'nt blind.

Therefore Akbar demanded to hang the culprit and rewarded the girl for her bravery for telling the truth even at the critical situation.

5. The Loyal Gardener

One day the Emperor Akbar stumbled on a rock in his garden. He was in a foul mood that day and the accident made him so angry that he ordered the gardener's arrest and execution.

The next day when the gardener was asked what his last wish was before he was hanged, he requested an audience with the emperor.

This wish was granted, but when the man neared the throne he loudly cleared his throat and spat at the emperor's feet.

The emperor was taken aback and demanded to know why he had done such a thing. The gardener had acted on Birbal's advice and now Birbal stepped forward in the man's defence.

"Your Majesty," he said, "there could be no person more loyal to you than this unfortunate man. Fearing that people would say you hanged him for a trifle, he has gone out of his way to give you a genuine reason for hanging him."

The emperor, realising that he had been about to do a great injustice, set the man free.

6. Birbal identifies a guest

Birbal had been invited to lunch by a rich man. Birbal went to the man's house and found him in a hall full of people. His host greeted him warmly.

"I did not know there would be so many guests," said Birbal who hated large gatherings.

"They are not guests," said the man. "They are my employees, all except one man. He is the only other guest here beside you."

Then a crafty look came on the man's face.

"Can you tell me which of them is the guest?" he asked.

"Maybe I could," said Birbal. "Talk to them as I observe them. Tell them a joke or something."

The man told a joke that Birbal thought was perhaps the worst he had heard in a long time. When he finished everyone laughed uproariously.

"Well," said the rich man. "I've told my joke. Now tell me who my other guest is."

Birbal pointed out the man to him.

"How did you know?" asked his host, amazed.

"Employees tend to laugh at any joke told by their employers," explained Birbal. "When I saw that this man was the only one not laughing at your joke, and in fact, looked positively bored, I at once knew he was your other guest."

7. Noble Beggar

Emperor Akbar asked Birbal if it was possible for a man to be the 'lowest' and the 'noblest' at the same time.

"It is possible," said Birbal.

"Then bring me such a person," said the emperor.

Birbal went out and returned with a beggar.

"He is the lowest among your subjects," he said, presenting him to Akbar.

"That might be true," said Akbar. "But I don't see how he can be the 'noblest'."

"He has been given the honour of an audience with the emperor," said Birbal. "That makes him the noblest among beggars."

8. Birbal denies a rumour

One day a man stopped Birbal in the street and began narrating his woes to him.

"I've walked twenty miles to see you," he told Birbal finally, "and all along the way people kept saying you were the most generous man in the country."

Birbal knew the man was going to ask him for money.

"Are you going back the same way?" he asked.

"Yes," said the man.

"Will you do me a favour?"

"Certainly," said the man. "What do you want me to do?"

"Please deny the rumour of my generosity," said Birbal, walking away.

9. Birbal outwits a cheat

A farmer and his neighbour once went to Emperor Akbar's court with a complaint.

"Your Majesty, I bought a well from him," said the farmer pointing to his neighbour," and now he wants me to pay for the water."

"That's right, your Majesty," said the neighbour. "I sold him the well but not the water!"

The Emperor asked Birbal to settle the dispute.

"Didn't you say that you sold your well to this farmer?" Birbal asked the neighbour. "So, the well belongs to him now, but you have kept your water in his well. Is that right? Well, in that case you will have to pay him a rent or take your water out at once."

The neighbour realised that he was outwitted. He quickly apologised and gave up his claim.

10. Birbal Shortens a Road

The emperor Akbar was travelling to a distant place along with some of his courtiers. It was a hot day and the emperor was tiring of the journey.

"Can't anybody shorten this road for me?" he asked, querulously.

"I can," said Birbal.

The other courtiers looked at one another, perplexed. All of them knew there was no other path through the hilly terrain. The road they were travelling on was the only one that could take them to their destination.

"You can shorten the road?" said the emperor. "Well, do it."

"I will," said Birbal. "Listen first to this story I have to tell."

And riding beside the emperor's palanquin, he launched upon a long and intriguing tale that held Akbar and all those listening, spellbound. Before they knew it they had reached the end of their journey.

"We've reached?" exclaimed Akbar. "So soon!"

"Well," grinned Birbal, "you did say you wanted the road to be shortened."

11. Birbal returns Home

Birbal was in Persia at the invitation of the king of that country. Parties were given in his honour and rich presents were heaped on him.

On the eve of his departure for home, a nobleman asked him how he would compare the king of Persia to his own king.

"Your king is a full moon," said Birbal. "Whereas mine could be likened to the quarter moon."

The Persians were very happy. But when Birbal got home he found that Emperor Akbar was furious with him.

"How could you belittle your own king!" demanded Akbar. "You are a traitor!"

"No, Your Majesty," said Birbal. "I did not belittle you. The full moon diminishes and disappears whereas the quarter moon grows from strength to strength. What I, in fact, proclaimed to the world is that your power is growing from day to day whereas that of the king of Persia is about to go into decline."

Akbar grunted in satisfaction and welcomed Birbal back with a warm embrace.

12. The Sharpest Sword and Shield

A man who made spears and shields once came to Akbar's court.

"Your Majesty, nobody can make shields and spears to equal mine," he said. "My shields are so strong that nothing can pierce them and my spears are so sharp that there's nothing they cannot pierce."

"I can prove you wrong on one count certainly," said Birbal suddenly.

"Impossible!" declared the man.

"Hold up one of your shields and I will pierce it with one of your spears," said Birbal with a smile.

13. Birbal's Choice

One day Emperor Akbar asked Birbal what he would choose if he were given a choice between justice and a gold coin.

"The gold coin," said Birbal.

Akbar was taken aback.

"You would prefer a gold coin to justice?" he asked, incredulously.

"Yes," said Birbal.

The other courtiers were amazed by Birbal's display of idiocy.

For years they had been trying to discredit Birbal in the emperor's eyes but without success and now the man had gone and done it himself!

They could not believe their good fortune.

"I would have been dismayed if even the lowliest of my servants had said this," continued the emperor. "But coming from you it's. . . it's shocking - and sad. I did not know you were so debased!"

"One asks for what one does not have, Your Majesty!" said Birbal, quietly. "You have seen to it that in our country justice is available to everybody. So as justice is already available to me and as I'm always short of money I said I would choose the gold coin."

The emperor was so pleased with Birbal's reply that he gave him not one but a thousand gold coins

14. Birbal, The Child

Birbal arrived late for a function and the emperor was displeased.

"My child was crying and I had to placate him," explained the courtier.

"Does it take so long to calm down a child?" asked the emperor. "It appears you know nothing about child rearing. Now you pretend to be a child and I shall act as your father and I will show you how you should have dealt with your child. Go on, ask me for whatever he asked of you."

"I want a cow," said Birbal.

Akbar ordered a cow to be brought to the palace.

"I want its milk. I want its milk," said Birbal, imitating the voice of a small child.

"Milk the cow and give to him," said Akbar to his servants.

The cow was milked and the milk was offered to Birbal. He drank a little and then handed the bowl back to Akbar.

"Now put the rest of it back into the cow, put it back, put in back, put it back..." wailed Birbal.

The emperor was flabbergasted and quietly left the room.

15. *Limping Horse*

A nobleman's prized racehorse began to limp for no apparent reason. Veterinarians who were called found nothing wrong with the leg - no fracture, no sprain, no soreness - and they were baffled.

The nobleman finally consulted a sage, a man known for his wisdom.

"Has anything changed for the horse in the last few months?" he asked.

"I changed his trainer a few weeks ago," said the nobleman.

"Does the horse get on well with his new trainer?"

"Very well! In fact, he's devoted to him."

"Does the trainer limp?"

"Uh... yes, he does."

"The reason for the horse's limp is clear," said the sage. "He's imitating his handler. We all tend to imitate those whom we admire. The company we keep has a great influence on us."

The nobleman put the horse in the charge of another trainer, and the horse soon stopped limping.

16. *The Emperor's Servant*

One day Akbar and Birbal were riding through the countryside and they happened to pass by a cabbage patch.

"Cabbages are such delightful vegetables!" said Akbar. "I just love cabbage."

"The cabbage is king of vegetables!" said Birbal.

A few weeks later they were riding past the cabbage patch again. This time however, the emperor made a face when he saw the vegetables.

"I used to love cabbage but now I have no taste for it." said Akbar.

"The cabbage is a tasteless vegetable" agreed Birbal.

The emperor was astonished.

"But the last time you said it was the king of vegetables!" he said.

"I did," admitted Birbal. "But I am your servant Your Majesty, not the cabbage's."

17. *Birbal, The Wise Judge*

Ramu and Shamu both claimed ownership of the same mango tree.

One day they approached Birbal and asked him to settle the dispute.

Birbal said to them: "There is only one way to settle the matter. Pluck all the fruits on the tree and divide them equally between the two of you. Then cut down the tree and divide the wood".

Ramu thought it was a fair judgement and said so.

But Shamu was horrified.

"Your Honour" he said to Birbal "I've tended that tree for seven years. I'd rather let Ramu have it than see it cut down."

"Your concern for the tree has told me all I wanted to know" said Birbal, and declared Shamu the true owner of the tree.

18. The True King

The King of Iran had heard that Birbal was one of the wisest men in the East and desirous of meeting him sent him an invitation to visit his country.

In due course, Birbal arrived in Iran.

When he entered the palace he was flabbergasted to find not one but six kings seated there.

All looked alike. All were dressed in kingly robes.

Who was the real king?

The very next moment he got his answer.

Confidently, he approached the king and bowed to him.

"But how did you identify me?" the king asked, puzzled.

Birbal smiled and explained: "The false kings were all looking at you, while you yourself looked straight ahead. Even in regal robes, the common people will always look to their king for support."

Overjoyed, the king embraced Birbal and showered him with gifts.

19. Question for Question

One day Akbar said to Birbal: "Can you tell me how many bangles your wife wears?"

Birbal said he could not.

"You cannot?" exclaimed Akbar. "You see her hands every day while she serves you food. Yet you do not know how many bangles she has on her hands? How is that?"

"Let us go down to the garden, Your Majesty," said Birbal, "and I'll tell you."

They went down the small staircase that led to the garden.

Then Birbal turned to the emperor: "Your Majesty," he said, "You go up and down this staircase every day. Can you tell me how many steps there are in the staircase?"

The emperor grinned sheepishly and quickly changed the subject.

20. Birbal's Painting

Once Akbar told Birbal 'Birbal, make me a painting. Use imagination in it. To which the reply was 'But hoozoor, I am a minister, how can I possibly paint?'.

The king was angry and said 'If I don't get a good painting by one week then you shall be hanged!'. The clever Birbal had an idea.

After one week, he went to the court and with him he carried a covered frame. Akbar was happy to see that Birbal had obeyed him, until he opened the cover.

The courtiers rushed to see what was wrong. What they saw made them feel very happy. At last, they would not see Birbal in court!

The painting was nothing but ground and sky. There were a few specs of green on the ground. The Emperor, angrily, told Birbal 'what is this!'

To which the reply was 'A cow eating grass hoozoor!'. Akbar said 'where is the cow and grass?' and Birbal told 'I used my imagination. The cow ate the grass and returned to its shed!'

21. Birbal betrays himself

Birbal was missing.

He and the emperor had a quarrel and Birbal had stormed out of the palace vowing never to return. Now Akbar missed him and wanted him back but no one knew where he was.

Then the emperor had a brainwave. He offered a reward of 1000 gold coins to any man who could come to the palace observing the following condition.

The man had to walk in the sun without an umbrella but he had to be in the shade at the same time.

"Impossible," said the people.

Then a villager came carrying a string cot over his head and claimed the prize.

"I've walked in the sun but at the same time I was in the shade of the strings of the cot," he said. It was a brilliant solution.

On interrogation the villager confessed that the idea had been suggested to him by a man living with him.

"It could only be Birbal!" said the emperor, delighted.

Sure enough it was Birbal and he and the emperor had a joyous reunion.

22. Birbal identifies the thief

One fine morning , a minister from Emperor Akbar's court had gathered in the assembly hall.

He informed the Emperor that all his valuables had been stolen by a thief the previous night.

Akbar was shocked to hear this beause the place where that minister lived was the safest place in the kingdom. He invited Birbal to solve the mystery.

Akbar said "It is definitely not possible for an outsider to enter into the minister's house and steal the valuables. This blunder is definitely committed only by another minister of that court."

Saying so he arranged for a donkey to be tied to a pillar . He ordered all the courtiers to lift the donkey's tail and say "I have not stolen."

Birbal added "Only then we can judge the culprit."

After everyone had finished, he asked the courtiers to show their palm to him. All the courtiers except Alim Khan had a black patch of paint on their palm.

Birbal had actually painted the donkey's tail with a black coat of paint. In the fright, the guilty minister did not touch the donkey's tail at all.

Thus Birbal once again proved his intelligence and was rewarded by the king with 1000 gold coins.

23. Just One Question

One Day a scholar came to the court of Emperor Akbar and challenged Birbal to answer his questions and thus prove that he was as clever as people said he was.

He asked Birbal: "Would you prefer to answer a hundred easy questions or just a single difficult one?"

Both the emperor and Birbal had had a difficult day and were impatient to leave.

"Ask me one difficult question," sad Birbal.

"Well, then, tell me," said the man, "which came first into the world, the chicken or the egg?"

"The chicken," replied Birbal.

"How do you know?" asked the scholar, a note of triumph in his voice.

"We had agreed you would ask only one question and you have already asked it" said Birbal and he and the emperor walked away leaving the scholar gaping.

24. Birbal's sweet reply

One day the Emperor Akbar startled his courtiers with a strange question.

"If somebody pulled my whiskers what sort of punishment should be given him?" he asked.

"He should be flogged!" said one courtier.

"He should be hanged!" said another.

"He should be beheaded!" said a third.

"And what about you, Birbal?" asked the emperor. "What do you think would be the right thing thing to do if somebody pulled my whiskers?"

"He should be given sweets," said Birbal.

"Sweets?" gasped the other couriers.

"Yes, said Birbal. "Sweets, because the only one who would dare pull His Majesty's whiskers is his grandson."

So pleased was the emperor with the answer that he pulled off his ring and gave it to Birbal as a reward.

25. Birbal is brief

One day Akbar asked his courtiers if they could tell him the difference between truth and falsehood in three words or less.

The courtiers looked at one another in bewilderment.

"What about you, Birbal?" asked the emperor. "I'm surprised that you too are silent."

"I'm silent because I want to give others a chance to speak," said Birbal.

"Nobody else has the answer," said the emperor. "So go ahead and tell me what the difference between truth and falsehood is — in three words or less."

"Four fingers" said Birbal

"Four fingers?" asked the emperor, perplexed.

"That's the difference between truth and falsehood, your Majesty," said Birbal. "That which you see with your own eyes is the truth. That which you have only heard about might not be true. More often than not, it's likely to be false."

"That is right," said Akbar. "But what did you mean by saying the difference is four fingers?'

"The distance between one's eyes and one's ears is the width of four fingers, Your Majesty," said Birbal, grinning.

26. The Well dispute

Once there was a complaint at King Akbar's court.

There were two neighbours who shared their garden. In that garden, there was a well that was possessed by Iqbal khan.

His neighbour, who was a farmer wanted to buy the well for irrigation purpose. Therefore they signed an agreement between them, after which the farmer owned the well.

Even after selling the well to the farmer, Iqbal continued to fetch water from the well. Angered by this, the farmer had come to get justice from King Akbar.

King Akbar asked Iqbal the reason for fetching water from the well even after selling it to the farmer. Iqbal replied that he had sold only the well to the farmer but not the water inside it.

King Akbar wanted Raja Birbal who was present in the court listening to the problem to solve the dispute. Birbal came forward and gave a solution.

He said " Iqbal, You say that you have sold only the well to the farmer. And you claim that the water is yours.

Then how come you can keep your water inside another person's well without paying rent?" Iqbal's trickery was countered thus in a tricky way. The farmer got justice and Birbal was fairly rewarded.

27. List of the blind

Once King Birbal questioned Raja Birbal if he knows the number of blind citizens of their kingdom.

Raja Birbal had requested Akbar to give him a week's time. The next day Raja Birbal was found to be mending shoes in the town market.

People were astonished to see Birbal doing such work.

Many of them started to question "Birbal!! What are you doing?" Once when he was asked this question by someone he started writing something.

It continued for a week when on the 7th day King Akbar himself asked Birbal the same question. Giving him no answer, Birbal reported at the court the next day and handed over a note to King Akbar.

Akbar read the note when he found that it was the big list of people who were blind. Emperor Akbar was stunned when he found his own name in the list.

Angered by this, Akbar asked Birbal the reason for writing his name in the list. Birbal said "O! My majesty! Like all other people you also saw me mending the slippers but you still asked me what I was doing. Therefore I had to include your name too."

Akbar started laughing at this and everyone enjoyed Birbal's sense of humour.

28. The Musical Genius

Famous musicians once gathered at Akbar's court for a competition.

The one who could capture a bull's interest was to be declared the winner.

One by one, they played the most heavenly music but the bull paid no attention. Then Birbal took the stage.

His music sounded like the droning of mosquitoes and the mooing of cows.

But to everyone's amazement the bull suddenly became alert and began to move in a lively manner.

Akbar declared Birbal the winner.

29. Birbal Turns the Tables

Emperor Akbar was narrating a dream. The dream began with Akbar and Birbal walking towards each other on a moonless night. It was so dark that they could not see each other - and they collided, and fell.

"Fortunately for me," said the Emperor. "I fell into a pool of payasam. But guess what Birbal fell into?"

"What, your Majesty?" asked the courtiers.

"A gutter!"

The court resounded with laughter. The emperor was thrilled that for once he had been able to score over Birbal. But Birbal was unperturbed.

"Your Majesty," he said when the laughter had died down. "Strangely, I too had the same dream. But unlike you I slept on till the end. When you climbed out of that pool of delicious payasam and I, out of that stinking gutter we found that there was no water with which to clean ourselves and so guess what we did?

"What?" asked the emperor, warily.

"We licked each other clean!"

The emperor became red with embarrassment and resolved never to try to get the better of Birbal again.

30. *The Jealous Courtiers*

One day Emperor Akbar was inspecting the law and order situation in the kingdom.

One of his ministers, who was jealous of Raja Birbal, complained that the Emperor gave importance only to Birbal's suggestions and all the other ministers were ignored.

Akbar wanted the minister to know how wise Birbal was.

There was a marriage procession going on. The Emperor ordered the minister to enquire whose marriage it was.

The minister found out and walked towards the Emperor wearing a proud expression on his face. Then the king called Birbal and asked him too to enquire whose marriage was going on.

When Birbal returned, Akbar asked the minister "Where are the couple going?" The minister said that the king had only asked him to enquire whose marriage was going on.

Then Akbar asked Birbal the same question. "O My Majesty! They are going to the city of Allahabad," replied Raja Birbal.

Now the King turned towards the minister and said, "Now do you understand why Birbal is more important to me? It is not enough if you complete a task. You have to use your intelligence to do a little more work.'

The minister's face fell. He had learnt the importance of being Birbal, the hard way.

III

HUMOROUS 11

1- *Flowers for the Emperor*

Emperor Akbar and some of his courtiers were strolling through the royal gardens.

"How beautiful is that flower, Man can never produce anything as beautiful as this?" said the court poet, drawing the emperor's attention to a flower growing on a bush."Man can sometimes produce more beautiful things," said Birbal. "I don't believe it!" said the emperor. "You are talking nonsense, Birbal!"

A few days later Birbal led a master craftsman of Agra into Akbar's presence. The man presented the emperor with an exquisite marble carving of a bouquet of flowers.

The emperor rewarded him with a thousand gold coins. Just then a small boy entered and gave Akbar a bunch of roses. Akbar thanked the boy and gave him a silver coin.

"So the carving was more beautiful than the real thing," said Birbal softly and the emperor realized with a start that once again he had played into the hands of his witty courtier.

2 - *Sweet Reply*

One day the Emperor Akbar startled his courtiers with a strange question. "If somebody pulled my mustache what sort of punishment should be given to him?" he asked.

"He should be flogged!" said one courtier.

"He should be hanged!" said another.

"He should be beheaded!" said a third.

"And what about you, Birbal?" asked the emperor. "What do you think would be the right thing thing to do if somebody pulled my mustache?"

"He should be given sweets," said Birbal. "Sweets?" gasped the other couriers.

"Yes, said Birbal. "Sweets, because the only one who would dare pull His Majesty's mustache is his grandson."

So pleased was the emperor with the answer that he pulled off his ring and gave it to Birbal as a reward.

3 - *Hasty Punishment*

Once when Akbar was riding near a mango grove, an arrow whizzed past him. His soldiers rushed into the grove and caught hold of the archer, a young man, and brought him before Akbar.

"Why did you try to kill me?" Akbar shouted at the youth. " Jahanpannah, I wasn't trying to kill you. I was only trying to knock the mango down with my arrow!" said the youth, who was already very afraid.

The king was too angry to listen to him. "Put him to death in the same manner he tried to kill me," he ordered to his soldiers.

Receiving the King's orders soldiers tied the youth to a mango tree and another steadied his bow and arrow to shoot him.

"This is not fair!" shouted Birbal who had been watching quietly. "If you want to shoot him the same way he tried to shoot the emperor, you will have to aim at the mango and the arrow will have to miss the mango and then strike him."

Akbar, who had calmed down by now, realized he had been unfair to the youth and ordered his soldiers to release him. The young man bowed and thanked the king & Birbal .

4- *Birbal solves the problem*

Several courtiers were vying for the post of royal advisor. The emperor told them that he would put them to the test and the one who passed the test would be appointed as the royal advisor.

Akbar then unfastened his waist cloth (Cloak) and lay on the floor. He then challenged the courtiers to cover him from head to toe with the cloak.

One by one the courtiers tried, but their attempts proved futile. If the head was covered, the feet remained exposed. Some even tried pulling and tugging at the coak but in vain.

Just then Birbal entered. The emperor asked Birbal if he could do it. Birbal took the cloak and then looked at the emperor lying on the floor.

"Jahanpannah, would you kindly draw up your knees?" he said. The emperor drew up his knees. Birbal then threw the cloak over him and it covered him from head to toe.

The courtiers, realizing that they had failed the test, quietly filed out of the room.

5- *How many crows in the Kingdom?*

Being Emperor Akbar's favorite minister, Birbal used to solve many of his problems.

One day Emperor Akbar and Birbal were taking a walk in the palace gardens. It was a nice summer morning and there were plenty of crows happily playing around . Akbar was enjoying seeing so many crows playing.

Suddenly, while watching the crows, a question came into Akbar's head. He wondered how many crows were there in his kingdom.

Since Birbal was accompanying him, he asked Birbal this question. Birbal looked at the crows and after a moment's thought, Birbal replied, "There are ninety-five thousand four hundred and sixty-three crows in the Kingdom".

Amazed by his quick response, Akbar tried to test him again, "What if there are more crows than you answered?"

Without hesitating Birbal replied, "If there are more crows than my answer, then some crows are visiting from other neighboring kingdoms".

"And what if there are less crows", Akbar asked. "Then some crows from our kingdom have gone on holidays to other places". Akbar was very much impressed at this intelligent answer from Birbal.

6- *Caught the Thief*

It so happened that once a rich merchant's house was robbed. The merchant suspected that the thief was one of his servants. So he went to Birbal and mentioned the incident. Birbal went to his house and assembled all of his servants and asked that who stole the merchant's things.

Everybody denied.

Birbal thought for a moment, then gave a stick of equal length to all the servants of the merchant and said to them that the stick of the real thief will be longer by two inches tomorrow. All the servants should be present here again tomorrow with heir sticks.

All the servants went to their homes and gathered again at the same place the next day. Birbal asked them to show him their sticks. One of the servants had his stick shorter by two inches.

Birbal said, "This is your thief, merchant."

Later the merchant asked Birbal, "How did you catch him?" Birbal said, "The thief had already cut his stick short by two inches in the night fearing that his stick will be longer by two inches by morning."

7- *Beautiful Explanation*

One day the Emperor Akbar saw a woman hugging and kissing a very dark, ugly and unattractive child. He was very surprised to see that. He thought and thought but could not think why?

He asked Birbal that why she was doing that to such an unattractive child. Birbal replied innocently, "Huzoor, he must have been her own child. For every mother her own child is the most beautiful child in the world."

The Emperor did not seem to be convinced with this explanation, and Birbal had guessed this from the Emperor's face.

Next day, in the presence of the Emperor, Birbal ordered a Guard to present the most beautiful child in the world in the court. Next day, the Guard brought a more unattractive and ugly child with buck teeth and his hair stood like a porcupine and presented to the Emperor. "This is the most beautiful child in the world, Your majesty." the Guard stammered.

The Emperor asked, "How do you know that he is the most beautiful child in the world?" "Your Majesty, I went home and posed my problem to my wife. She told me to bring our child to the court." the Guard replied meekly.

8- *The Sadhu*

Akbar came to the throne when he was only thirteen years old. In the years that followed, he built on of the greatest empires of his time. He lived in unimaginable splendor. He was surrounded by courtiers who agreed with every word he said, who flattered him and treated him as if he were a god. Perhaps it was not surprising that Emperor Akbar was sometimes arrogant and behaved as if the whole world belonged to him.

One day, Birbal decided to make the great emperor stop and think about life.

That evening as the emperor was going towards his palace, he noticed a Sadhu lying in the centre of his garden. He could not believe his eyes. A strange Sadhu, in ragged clothes, right in the middle of the palace garden? The guards would have to be punished for this, thought the emperor furiously as he walked over to that Sadhu and prodded him with the tip of his embroidered slipper.

"Here, fellow!" he cried. "What are you doing here? Get up and go away at once!"

That Sadhu opened his eyes. Then he sat up slowly. "Huzoor," he said in a sleepy voice. "Is this your garden, then?"

"Yes!" cried the Emperor. "This garden those rose bushes, the fountain beyond that, the courtyard, the palace, this fort, this empire, it all belongs to me!"

Slowly that Sadhu stood up. "And the river, Huzoor? And the city? And this country?"

"Yes, yes, it's all mine", said the emperor. "Now get out!"

"Ah", said the Sadhu. "And before you, Huzoor. Who did the garden and fort and city belong to then?"

"My father, of course", said the emperor. In spite of his irritation, he was beginning to get interested in the Sadhu's questions. He loved philosophical discussions and he could tell, from his manner of speaking, that the Sadhu was a learned man.

"And who was here before him?" the Sadhu asked quietly.

"His father, my father's father, as you know."

"Ah", said the Sadhu. So this garden, those rose bushes, the palace and the fort all this has only belonged to you for your lifetime. Before that they belonged to your father, am I right? And after yours time they will belong to your son, and then to his son?

"Yes", said the Emperor Akbar wonderingly.

"So each one stays here for a time and then goes on his ways?"

"Yes."

"Like a dharmashala?" the Sadhu asked. "No one owns a dharmashala. Or the shade of a tree on the side of a road. We stop and rest for a while and then go on. And someone has always been there before us and someone will always come after we have gone. Is that not so?"

"It is", Emperor Akbar quietly.

"So your garden, your palace, your fort, your empire... these are only places you will stay in for a time, for the span of your lifetime. When you die, they will no longer belong to you. You will go, leaving them in the possession of someone else, just as your father did and his father before him."

Emperor Akbar nodded. "The whole world is a dharmashala", he said slowly, thinking very hard. "In which we mortals rest awhile. That's what you are telling me, isn't it? Nothing on this earth can ever belong to a single person, because each person is only passing through the earth and must die one day?"

The Sadhu nodded solemnly. Then, bowing to the ground, he removed his white beard and saffron turban and his voice changed. "Jahanpanah, forgive me!" he said, in his normal voice. "It was my way of asking you to think about..."

"Birbal, oh, Birbal!" the emperor exclaimed. "You are wiser than any philosopher. Come, come at once to the royal chamber and let us discuss this further. Even emperors are but wayfarers on the path of life, it is clear!"

9- *Heavy Burden*

Once a distraught old woman came to Birbal for help. The emperor had decided to build a palace on her property. She didn't want to leave the place as it had been her ancestral property. Birbal assured her and said that he'd do his best.

The construction began. When Birbal visited the site with Akbar, he saw many gunny bags lying next to a pile of mud. He began to fill the bags with mud.

"Why are you doing this?" asked Akbar. "To earn merit in my next life, Huzoor," replied Birbal.

Amused, Akbar too joined Birbal. Afterwards Birbal requested Akbar to help him lift one of the sacks.

"Aaah, this is very heavy!" said Akbar, staggering under the weight of a bag. "Your Majesty," said Birbal, "A bag of mud is so heavy. Imagine how much mud there must be in this piece of land. Will it not weigh heavily on your conscience to destroy somebody ancestral property?"

Akbar realized his mistake and gave orders to discontinue the construction.

10- *Pundit's Mother Tongue*

Once Akbar's court was visited by an eminent Pundit who was well versed in many languages. He challenged everybody in the Court that he could answer any question in any languages. No doubt he used to answer queries in whichever language he was asked. Nobody could guess his true mother tongue.

He once said to Emperor Akbar that by tomorrow your courtier's should tell me which is my mother tongue and if they failed to do so, I assume that I am superior than all your courtiers.

Everyone in the court thought it to be an easy job and pleaded their inability to judge his mother tongue. But everyone failed now Akbar turned to Birbal to solve this problem. Birbal accepted the challenge and asked for some time till the next morning. Time was granted & the durbar (social gathering) was dismissed.

That night Birbal went to Pundit's house and entered his bedroom. When the Pundit was fast asleep Birbal tickled his ear with hay (dry Grass).

The Pundit's sleep was disturbed, he turned to the other side and slept, again Birbal tickled his other ear. Now Pundit's sleep was disturbed he woke up and loudly said "Yevvurura Adi" (Who is that?) and seeing no one he went back to sleep. Birbal came out of his house unnoticed.

The next morning, the court assembled, and the Pundit was also invited. Pundit again started in different languages, finally Birbal said that 'TELUGU' is the mother tongue of the Pundit. The Pundit was very much surprised at Birbal's answer and he accepted the defeat and left the court.

Akbar asked Birbal, how he found out the true mother tongue. Birbal said that a man in distress will talk in his mother tongue whenever he is disturbed in sleep and then narrated the happening of the previous night. Akbar praised Birbal for his timely Wisdom.

11- *What the drop Taketh*

The anecdotes of Emperor Akbar and his trusted aide Birbal are entertaining as well as enlightening. Once, the Emperor received the gift of a rare perfume. As he opened the bottle, a drop of perfume fell to the floor.

Akbar instinctively moved to retrieve it by wiping the floor with his finger. As he looked up he noticed a bemused look on Birbal's face... his eyes seemed to mock the Emperor for being scrounging.

To change Birbal's perception, Akbar summoned him the next morning to his bath. He asked his attendants to fill up the bathtub with the best of perfumes. Akbar sought to show Birbal that as Emperor he could afford to waste as much perfume, as he wanted. Birbal when asked to react said the immortal lines, "Boond se jati, woh haudh se nahi aati" (An entire tub full cannot retrieve what the drop took way!)

Birbal sought to tell the Emperor that his earlier instinctive action (that exhibited miserliness) could not be undone by an intentional action (aimed at big-heartedness). Our character is determined by our reactions, not by forced posturing. It is better to be transparent then wear favourable masks. In fact every little action and reaction, every spoken word and emerging thought reflects our true self!